The Snowman ™

Der Schneemann

PIANO SCORE

———◆———

Music & Words by
Howard Blake

based on the picture book by
Raymond Briggs

CHESTER MUSIC

Published by
CHESTER MUSIC LIMITED

Exclusive Distributors:
HAL LEONARD
7777 West Bluemound Road,
Milwaukee, WI 53213
Email: info@halleonard.com

HAL LEONARD EUROPE LIMITED
42 Wigmore Street Marylebone,
London, W1U 2 RN
Email: info@halleonardeurope.com

HAL LEONARD AUSTRALIA PTY. LTD.
4 Lentara Court Cheltenham,
Victoria, 9132 Australia
Email: info@halleonard.com.au

Order No. CH76879
ISBN: 978-1-84938-560-2

The Snowman is recorded complete on Sony 71116.
The sheet music of *Walking in the Air* is available separately: CH77110.

THE SNOWMAN

Der Schneemann

HOWARD BLAKE

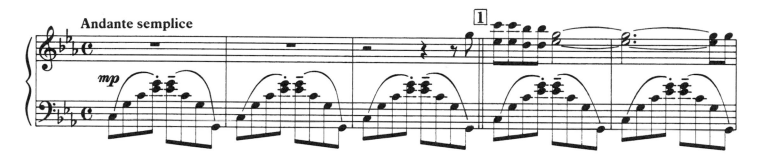

It was a cold, cold winter's night. In a cottage in the country, tucked
Es war eine kalte, kalte Winternacht. In einem Häuschen auf dem Land,

away beneath the hills, a little boy lay sleeping. Snow began to fall, lightly at first and then with giant flakes, which
tief versteckt zwischen den Hügeln, schlief ein kleiner Junge. Schnee begann zu fallen, anfangs leicht and dann mit Riesenflocken,

started to settle on the ground.
die auf der Erde liegen blieben.

At first light of morning, the little boy
turned over, yawned and sat up.
*Beim ersten Morgenstrahl drehte sich der
kleine Junge um, gähnte und setzte sich auf.*

He ran to the window and looked out.
Er rannte ans Fenster und sah hinaus.

Everything was covered in snow...
Alles war voll Schnee...

the garden, the fields and the distant hills.
der Garten, die Wiesen und die Hügel in der Ferne.

He got dressed
as fast as he could.
*So schnell wie er
konnte zog er sich an.*

When he was ready, he
hurried down the stairs.
*Als er fertig war, rannte
er die Stiege hinunter.*

At the back door he put on his boots, his scarf and his woolly hat and walked out into the snow.
An der Hintertür zog er seine Stiefel an, seinen Schal und seine wollene Mütze und stapfte hinaus in den Schnee.

First of all, he thought,
I'll make some giant footsteps.
Zuerst einmal, dachte er, werde ich ein paar riesige Fußstapfen machen.

Tranquillo subito

5 **Alla marcia, pesante**

Above him was a branch of a tree.
Über ihm war der Ast eines Baumes.

He jumped up and swung on it.
Er sprang hoch und schwang an ihm.

The snow from the branch fell all over him.
Der Schnee von dem Ast machte ihn ganz weiß.

Then he made a snowball and threw it as hard as he possibly could…
Dann drehte er einen Schneeball und warf ihn so fest er konnte…

straight into the kitchen window.
gerade ins Küchenfenster.

'You do something else',
said his mother.
*'Mach' was anderes',
sagte seine Mutter.*

heavy

4

The little boy wandered off,
wondering what to do.
*Der kleine Junge ging weg und
wußte nicht, was er tun sollte.*

And it was at exactly this moment that he
got the idea of building the snowman.
*Und da fiel ihm plötzlich ein,
daß er einen Schneemann baute.*

He built a great column of
snow the size of a man...
*Er baute eine große Säule aus
Schnee, groß wie ein Mann...*

and a great big snowball
to go on top of it.
*und einen großen dicken
Schneeball oben drauf.*

Then he fetched a scarf and a hat,
a tangerine for the nose, and coal for the eyes.
*Dann holte er einen Schal und einen Hut, eine
Mandarine für die Nase und Kohlen für die Augen.*

At last the snowman was finished, and
the boy stepped back and looked at him.
Endlich war der Schneeman fertig und
der Junge trat zurück und sah ihn an.

He seemed to be smiling.
Sein Gesicht schien zu lächeln.

By this time it was getting dark
and the little boy had to go indoors,
Nun werde es dunkel, der kleine
Junge mußte ins Haus zurück,

leaving the snowman standing all alone,
out in the middle of the garden.
und der Schneemann blieb ganz allein,
draußen mitten im Garten.

He went back to bed, but
then the clock woke him.
*Er kroch zurück ins Bett,
dann weckte ihn die Uhr.*

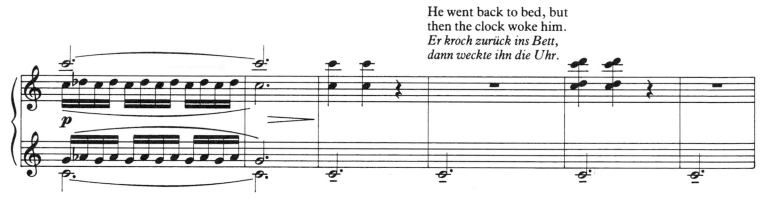

This time he got up and tiptoed down the stairs, feeling rather cold.
Diesmal stand er auf und schlich die Stiege hinunter, es war ihm recht kalt.

He looked out at the snowman through the glass panels of the front door.
Durch das Glas der Haustür schaute er zum Schneeman hinaus.

Suddenly, while the boy was looking at him, the snowman...   moved!
Plötzlich, als ihn der Junge ansah,   bewegte sich der Schneemann!

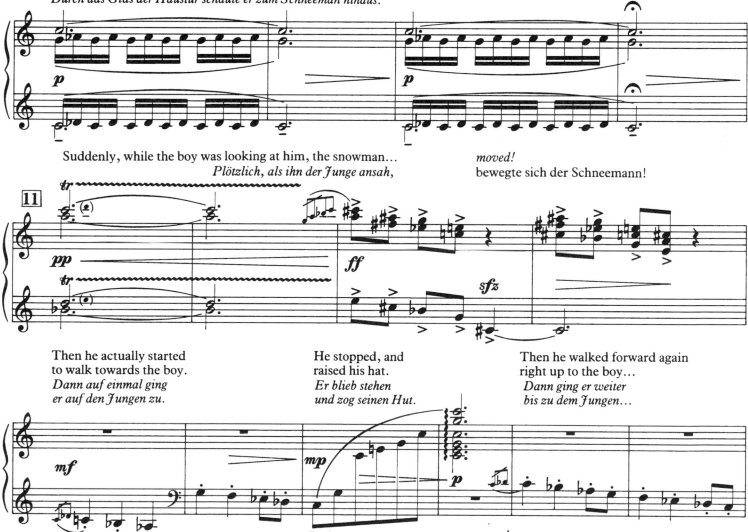

Then he actually started   He stopped, and   Then he walked forward again
to walk towards the boy.   raised his hat.   right up to the boy...
Dann auf einmal ging   *Er blieb stehen*   *Dann ging er weiter*
er auf den Jungen zu.   *und zog seinen Hut.*   *bis zu dem Jungen...*

and they shook hands.
*und sie gaben
einander die Hand.*

'Come in?',
said the boy.
*'Komm herein?',
sagte der Junge.*

'I'd love to',
said the snowman.
*'Mit Vergnügen',
sagte der Schneemann.*

Together they tiptoed into the living room.
Zusammen gingen sie auf Zehenspitzen ins Wohnzimmer.

The snowman thought it was wonderful.
Der Schneemann fand das herrlich.

He looked at the cat sleeping peacefully by the fire, and wanted to stroke it.
Er sah die Katze friedlich am Kamin schlafen und wollte sie streicheln.

But when the cat saw the
snowman, he was terrified
*Als aber die Katze den
Schneemann sah, erschrak sie*

and leapt into the air. The snowman jumped
backwards and lurched into the Christmas tree,
*und sprang in die Luft. Der Schneemann trat
hastig zurück und stieß an den Christbaum*

setting all the little bells ringing, the candles shaking and the fairy wobbling.
und all die Glöckchen läuteten, die Kerzen zitterten und der Engel auf der Spitze wackelte.

At last it settled down and the boy plugged it in.
*Als der Baum wieder stillestand,
knipste der Junge den Schalter an.*

The tree lit up with every colour you could think of—
Der Baum erstrahlte mit allen Farben, die man sich denken kann— blau und grün,

blues and greens,

But his own tangerine fitted best, so he put it back on.
Seine eigene Mandarine paßte aber am besten und so steckte er sie wieder zurück.

He leaned down and opened the fridge, and a waft of cold air came out.
Er bückte sich nieder, machte den Kühlschrank auf und eine Welle kalter Luft kam heraus.

The snowman loved it.
Das gefiel dem Schneemann.

For him it was just like sunbathing.
Für ihn war es wie ein Sonnenbad.

Alla Calypso

'Let's go upstairs', said the boy. Up they went and paused outside his parents' room. Someone was snoring.
'Laß uns hinaufgehen', sagte der Junge. Sie stiegen hinauf und blieben vor dem Schlafzimmer der Eltern stehen. Jemand schnarchte.

poco rit.

Ped._____ | Ped._____|

'Be very quiet', said the boy.
'Sei ganz still', sagte der Junge.

'Sshhh!'
'schschsch!'

'Look–false teeth', whispered the boy.
'Schau–ein Gebiß', flüsterte der Junge.

The snowman wanted to try them on.
Der Schneemann wollte es anprobieren.

He put them on and walked to a mirror to see how they looked.
Er steckte es in den Mund und schaute in den Spiegel.

It gave him a terrible fright.
Es jagte ihm einen fürchtlichen Schrecken ein.

white note gliss.

He held his nose.
Er hielt sich die Nase zu.

He mustn't sneeze
in the bedroom.
*Er darf im Schlafzimmer
nicht niesen.*

The boy hurried him
out of the room…
*Der Junge schob ihn
rasch aus dem Zimmer…*

and then…
dann…

he sneezed!
nieste er!

In the boy's playroom
was a music box.
*Im Zimmer des Jungen
war eine Spieldose.*

MUSIC-BOX DANCE
Der Spieldosentanz

Tempo di Valse

They wound it up and danced to it.
Sie zogen sie auf und tanzten danach.

At the end of the dance they both collapsed onto the floor, with balloons and teddy bears all around them.
Als der Tanz vorüber war, fielen sie beide auf den Boden, und um sie herum waren lauter Ballons und Teddybären.

'I've got another idea now', said the boy.   'Come with me and look out of the window'.
'Jetzt habe ich eine andere Idee', sagte der Junge.   *'Komm mit mir und schau zum Fenster hinaus.'*

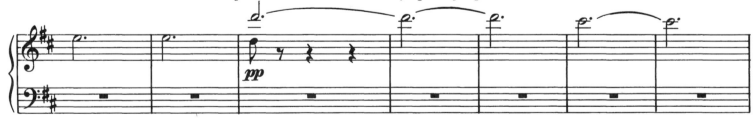

Outside they could see a strange dark object.
Draußen konnten sie ein sonderbares dunkles Ding sehen.

Nodding to each other, they
tiptoed silently down the stairs,
*Sie nickten einander zu und schlichen
lautlos die Stiege hinunter,*

out through the front door
and into the open air.
*hinaus durch die
Vordertür und ins Freie.*

The dark object seemed much bigger now they were close to it,
and whatever it was was covered up with a big black tarpaulin.
*Das dunkle Ding sah aus der Nähe viel großer aus und, was immer es
auch war, es war mit einer großen schwarzen Zeltplane zugedeckt.*

Summoning up all his strength,
the boy went up and pulled it off.
*Der Junge nahm all seine Kraft
zusammen, ging hin und zog sie herunter.*

MOTOR BIKE GALOP
Die Motorradjagd

Standing there was a bright...
Da stand ein helles...

shiny new motor bike.
glänzendes neues Motorrad.

The boy pointed out the controls to the snowman,
Der Junge zeigte dem Schneemann die Schalter,

turned the key in the ignition,
drehte den Zündschlüssel herum,

turned on the headlight,
knipste die Scheinwerfer an,

and suddenly the snowman was on the bike and racing round the garden.
und plötzlich saß der Schneemann auf dem Motorrad und raste im Garten herum.

For a second he stopped; the little boy
Eine Sekunde lang stoppte er; der kleine Junge schwang

jumped on behind him and then…they were off!
sich auf den Rücksitz und dann… sausten sie los!

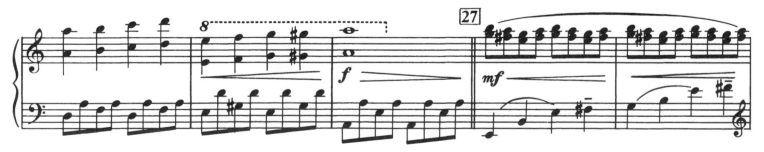

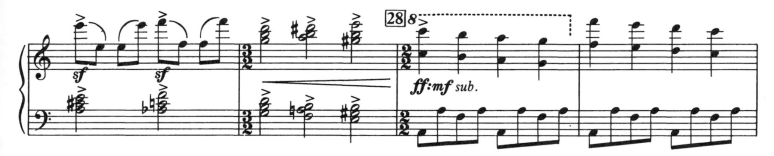

When they came back to the garden,
Als sie in den Garten zurückkamen,

the snowman found his legs had started to melt from the heat of the engine. He was dripping all over the place, as if he'd just come
sah der Schneeman, daß seine Beine in der Hitze des Motors schmolzen. Rundherum tröpfelte er, als ob er gerade aus der Badewanne käme.

out of the bath tub.   At that moment the boy had another bright idea.   Grabbing the snowmans' hand,
In diesen Augenblick hatte der Junge eine andere Idee.   Er nahm den Schneemann bei der

he pulled him into the garage.   Humming away in the corner was the big deep freeze.
Hand und zog ihn in die Garage.   In der Ecke brummte die Tiefkühltruhe vor sich hin.

In a second the snowman had jumped into the freezer, and in another second the dripping had...   stopped!
In Sekundenschnelle war der Schneemann in die Truhe gesprungen,   und nach einer weiteren Sekunde hatte das Tröpfeln... aufgehört.

The little boy
watched him lying there,
*Der kleine Junge sah
ihn an, wie er dort lag,*

and realised that an idea had come into the snowman's head.   Without warning the snowman climbed out of the freezer and,
und bemerkte, daß dem Schneemann etwas eingefallen war.   Ohne Warnung kletterte der Schneeman aus der Kühltruhe,

gripping the boy firmly by the hand, began to run...
faßte den Jungen fest bei der Hand und fing an zu rennen...

out of the garage,
aus der Garage,

out into the snow,
hinaus in den Schnee,

out across the garden,
hinaus durch den Garten

faster and faster,
schneller und schneller,

bounding and jumping,
hüpfend und springend,

until suddenly the boy realised that they were...
bis der Junge plötzlich merkete, daß sie...

flying!....
flogen!....

SONG: 'WALKING IN THE AIR'
Lied: 'Wandern durch die Luft'

♩=96   SOLO BOY SOPRANO

We're walk-ing in the air, _____ we're
Wir wan-dern durch die Luft, _____ Wir

float-ing in the moon – lit sky; _____ the peo-ple far be-low are
schwe-ben auf'nem Mon – den-strahl, _____ Nun in der Fer-ne drun – ten

sleep-ing as we fly. _____ I'm hold-ing ve-ry tight, _____ I'm
schla-fen Berg und Tal. _____ *Ich hal-te im-mer fest* _____ *zum*

B♭ Dm

rid-ing in the mid — night blue; _____ I'm find-ing I can fly so
Rei-ten durch das dun — kle Blau, _____ *Die Land-schaft un-ten flik — kert*

C Gm

33

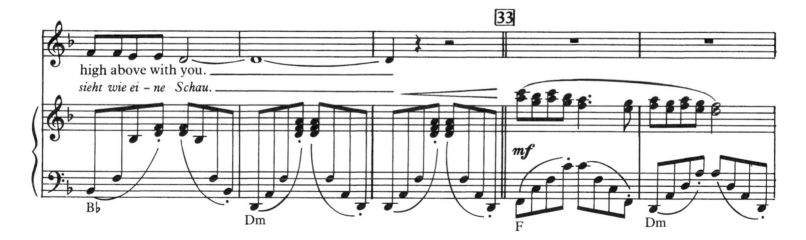

high above with you. _____
sieht wie ei — ne Schau. _____

mf

B♭ Dm F Dm

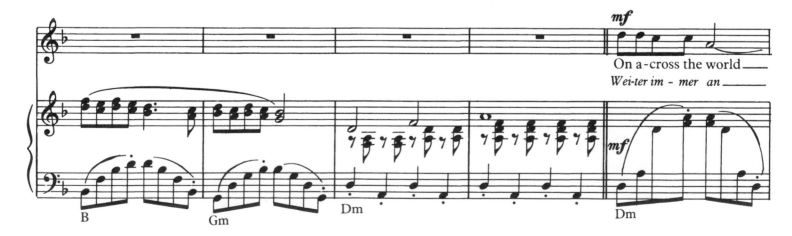

mf

On a-cross the world ___
Wei-ter im — mer an ___

B Gm Dm Dm

mf

the vil-la-ges go by like dreams,_____ the ri-vers and the hills, the
die Dör-fer se-geln sanft vor-bei._____ *Die Flüs-se und die Wäl - der*

34

fo-rests and the streams._____ Child-ren gaze
al - le träu-mend frei._____ *Kin-der starr'n,*

o-pen mouthed, ta-ken by sur - prise; no-bo-dy
höchst er-staunt *Könn' es kaum ver - steh'n.* *Off-ne Mun - - de,*

35

down be-low be - lieves their eyes. We're surf-ing in the air,_____
wei-te Au - - gen uns zu seh'n. *Wir schwim-men ohn' Ge-räusch,_____*

we're swimming in the fro — zen sky,_____ we're

wir sur-fen in der kla — ren Luft,_____ *zum*

C

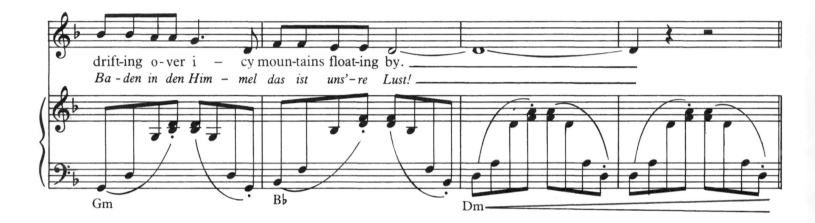

drift-ing o-ver i — cy moun-tains float-ing by. _____

Ba-den in den Him — mel das ist uns'-re Lust! _____

Gm   B♭   Dm

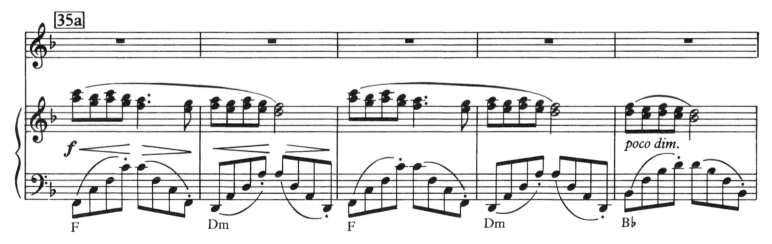

35a

f   *poco dim.*

F   Dm   F   Dm   B♭

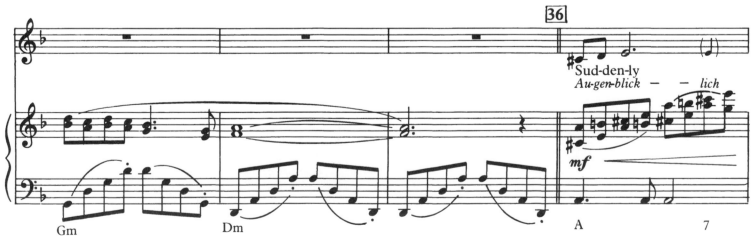

36

Sud-den-ly   (♩)

Au-gen-blick — — lich

mf

Gm   Dm   A   7

swoop-ing low on an o — — cean deep, rous-ing up a
flie-gen tief zu 'nem dun — — klen Meer. Wir zu wek — — ken

Dm 7 G 7 C Cm 7

migh-ty mon — — ster from his sleep; We're
von dem Schlaf ein Un — — ge — heu'r. Wir

F 7 B♭ E7 A

[37]

walk-ing in the air, We're danc-ing in the mid — night sky
tan-zen in der Höh'. Wir wan-dern durch die dun — kle Luft,

Dm C

and ev-ery-one who sees us greets us as we fly.
und wer uns so be-merkt ganz herz — lich uns be-grüsst.

Gm B♭ Dm

[38] They landed silently in the frozen North.
Lautlos landeten sie im eisigen Norden.

Poco misterioso (faster)

They were in the middle of a great
forest of pine trees, laden with snow.
*Sie waren inmitten eines großen Walds
von Fichten, die schwer waren von Schnee.*

But somewhere ahead they could
hear music and see lights.
*Von irgendwo in der Ferne
kam Musik und man sah Lichter.*

There in a clearing in the forest a Christmas party was taking place, and all the people
Dort fand auf einer Lichtung im Wald eine Weinachtsfeier statt, und alle Gäste bei der Feier

at the party were snowmen–more snowmen than you could ever imagine in your life.
waren Schneemänner–mehr Schneemänner als man sich je vorstellen kann.

And there, right in the middle of them,
radiating good cheer and smiling from
[39] **Solemn**
*Und dort, genau in der Mitte, stand
voll Frölichkeit und mit einem*

ear to ear, was Father Christmas himself. 'You're just in time for the Dance of the Snowmen', he chuckled… and clicked his fingers.
breiten Lachen, der Weihnachtsmann selbst. 'Ihr kommt eben zurecht zum Schneemännertanz', gluckste er… und schnalzte mit den Fingern.

DANCE OF THE SNOWMEN
Der Schneemännertanz

When the party was all over, Father Christmas led the boy and the snowman to a stable.
Als die ganze Feier vorüber war, führte der Weinachtsmann den Jungen und den Schneemann zu einem Stall.

l'istesso tempo

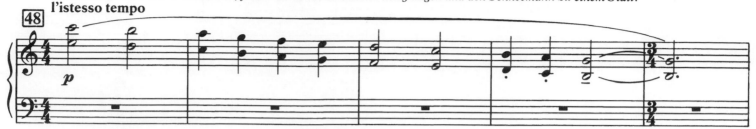

Light spilled through the door, and inside they could see the reindeer which he used to pull his sleigh.
Durch die Tür fiel Licht und drinnen konnten sie das Rentier sehen, das seinen Schlitten zog.

Father Christmas gave the boy a lovely blue scarf as a present, and he put it on.
Der Weinachtsmann gab dem Jungen einen hübschen blauen
Schal als Geschenk und der Junge hängte ihn um.

It was time for them to go.
Nun war es Zeit zu gehen.

The snowman gripped the boy's hand,
and once again they started to run…
Der Schneemann faßte den Jungen bei
der Hand und dann rannten sie wieder…

faster and faster… bounding and jumping until they were flying!
schneller und schneller… hüpfend und springend…bis sie flogen!

At last they landed in the garden again,
and together walked slowly to the house.
*Endlich landeten sie wieder im Garten
und gingen zusammen langsam zum Haus.*

50

The little boy shook hands with the
snowman and went up to the front door.
*Der kleine Junge drückte dem Schneemann
die Hand und ging zur Eingangstür.*

But the snowman waved, and the boy
ran back and gave him a great big hug.
*Doch der Schneemann winkte und der Junge lief
zurück und gab ihm einen großen dicken Gutenachtkuß.*

Then the boy went indoors, and very soon was fast asleep.
Dann ging der Junge ins Haus, und war gleich fest eingeschlafen.

51 Vivo

Next morning when he woke the room was ablaze with sunlight.
Als er am nächsten Morgen erwachte, schien die Sonne hell ins Zimmer.

He put on his dressing gown,
Er zog seinen Schlafrock an,

ran downstairs and opened the front door.
rannte hinunter und machte die Haustür auf.

The sun felt warm on his face.   The boy
Warm schien die Sonne auf sein Gesicht.   Der Junge

ran out into the
garden and saw…
rannte hinaus in
den Garten und sah…

a little heap of melted snow, an old hat, a tangerine, a scarf
and a few lumps of coal… But the snowman was nowhere to be seen
einen kleinen Haufen geschmolzenen Schnee, einen alten Hut, eine Mandarine, einen Schal
und ein paar Kohlestückchen… Der Schneemann aber war nirgendwo zu sehen

For a moment he thought that the adventures of
the night before had been nothing but a dream.
Einen Augenblick lang dachte er, die Abenteuer der
letzten Nacht seien nichts gewesen als ein Traum.

But then he felt in his pocket, and the scarf that
Father Christmas had given him… was still…*there.*
Doch dann griff er in die Tasche, und der Schal, den ihm
der Weinachtsmann gegeben hatte… war noch…da.